THE ODIOUS ORPHANAGE OF PAPE CITY

Srikar Chitta

Clever Fox
PUBLISHING

Chennai • Bangalore

CLEVER FOX PUBLISHING
Chennai, India

Published by CLEVER FOX PUBLISHING 2022
Copyright © Srikar Chitta 2022

All Rights Reserved.
ISBN: 978-93-56480-52-0

CONTENTS

CHAPTER I

INTRODUCTION TO MY NIGHTMARE

It was a dark, dusty, and gloomy day. A dilapidated old house with barely any windows looked upon me. It felt as if this was a 300-year-old building—because it was. The doors were made of wood that was already rotten, and the wind made them creak forward and backward as if some madman was slamming them repeatedly. On top of the building, a rusty iron sign that read "*House of Victory, outside Pape City*" was the first introduction to my new home. A home with no parents, no siblings—a house full of children who did not know each other. But they all had one thing in common: they were all orphans, just like me.

Yes! You read it right. I am Chris, and I was 12 years old when I entered this nightmare house. My neighbors had shifted me here when my last living relative—my dearest grandfather—left this world. I had never seen my parents;

my dad perished in a small rebellion against the dictator, six months before I was born, and my mom passed away when she gave birth to me. My grandfather had raised me on his own.

When I walked into the house, it was already lunchtime. A boy in his late teens dragged me to the lunchroom, which was tiny. As I looked around nervously, someone threw a bowl full of potato soup at my face. Most of it landed on my shirt, but nobody cared. The soup tasted awful, and I felt I would die drinking it. I noticed that the lunch lady was having tomato soup and asked for that. As soon as I asked that, the lunch lady started screaming as if the world was ending.

"Who do you think you are? Do you think this is a five-star lunch buffet! Finish the potato soup fast! FINISH IT!"

After that horrible moment, she continued drinking her delicious tomato soup and tucking into a plate full of chicken. The aroma made me go crazy. This was my first sight of the evilest person on the planet. She had a pimple on the tip of her nose and a giant mole on her right cheek that made her look much eviler. She had a broad forehead and wide eyes with a terrifying unibrow. Her hair was short and so scant that she was almost bald. Her nails were so long that a lion would feel jealous. Her entire personality made me shiver to my bones. Her tone was rough; a child next to me whispered to me that when she screamed, her voice could be heard for miles around. If a newborn child listened to her voice, the child would cry for a week and no one could calm it down. Her voice was so frightening and bone-chilling that even wolves, lions, and other predatory animals would run away if they heard it.

"Stop gossiping! Or else I will feed you two to the vultures!" she screamed.

I wondered how everyone in this orphanage lived with such a villainous personality. All the other kids were quietly drinking what they had been served. But looking at the lunch lady's plate, I was outraged.

I shouted, "*Can anyone in this world survive after drinking this awful soup? Is this an orphanage or a human prison cell? Why is nobody questioning this?*"

Hearing this, the lunch lady smiled wickedly and hollered for a boy named Seth. I thought, *Who is this Seth, and what is he going to do with me?* Then the same teenage boy who had dragged me into the lunchroom came with an evil grin on his face, as if he wanted to tear me apart like a lion looking at his next meal of tasty zebra. In this case, he was the lion and I was the zebra.

He looked much wickeder than the lunch lady. His giant stature almost had me worried. His hair hung limply to his shoulders and he was enormously fat. While he was walking, I could feel the room shaking like there was an earthquake. I clearly understood from the way he walked that he had been trained by the lunch lady to punish the kids. He had a gold tooth, which made him look a lot like a pirate. His upper teeth were not evenly spaced; each tooth looked as if it was running away from his mouth. His lower teeth were hidden behind his lip. This alignment made him speak awkwardly.

The lunch lady turned to Seth. "*Seth, did you see? We have a new HERO in our orphanage! Take him to the Slime Room immediately and serve him what he deserves. Keep him in the tub of slime and cover his body completely with slime. Don't bring him out of the Slime Room until he understands that no one has the right to speak under me, as I am the most loyal, obedient, and sincere servant of the Supreme Commander of this glorious country of Hemasise.*"

All the other kids were listening and, on hearing the punishment, started chirping like excited birds. I felt disgusted thinking about slime.

Seth replied, "*Yes, madam. I will serve him the world's best treatment, which he deserves, on your command.*"

Not wasting a second, he dragged me out of the lunchroom, down the hallway, and into a narrow corridor. I was being squeezed between Seth and the wall, but he didn't care. He pushed me into a room where a large tub was filled with slime.

Seth said, "*As you're a HERO and you are new, I would like to go easy on you instead of locking you in a rat cellar for a week.*" He picked up a bottle of smelly liquid. "*I will give you two options. One, go into the tub, to which I will add this smelly liquid. Or, two, drink the smelly liquid. So, Chris, choose wisely.*" As I started thinking over the options, he laughed wickedly. "*Of course there is no option of choosing punishments for you! You only have the choice of bearing the horrible smell. I tricked ya … ha! You wanted to choose, ha ha!*"

Seth pushed me into the tub of slime and put the smelly liquid in a dispenser and squirted it on me, which almost made me vomit. I felt like my stomach would burst like a ticking time bomb. I asked, "How long do I have to stay in this tub?"

Seth sneered. "See, you twerp, stop asking dumb questions and try to understand that, in this orphanage, you have to obey Lamia's orders and then my orders. I might set you free if you serve me—or I might not." He started cackling.

I didn't know what liquid he had added to the slime, but I felt nauseous. *Who's Lamia?* I thought fuzzily. After a few minutes, I was unconscious. When I woke up, I was in a bed and I realized it was the next day. I saw two bright eyes staring at me from the adjacent bed as if I were a celebrity.

I mustered some energy and asked the boy, *"Why am I in a bed? Who are you, and why are you staring at me like that? It is so embarrassing. Can you please look away?"*

But he answered my polite request in the complete opposite way. *"Look, newbie. You want to know who I am? Listen, I am Natas, and I don't want you next to me."* He pulled out my luggage from under my bed and threw it out of the window. All the children in the dormitory cheered and encouraged him as if he had won a war. No one stood up for me.

Natas was short, and he had a sort of snout. Somehow, I liked the way his eyes looked—they were a brilliant blue. He had pitch-black skin as if he had touched the sun and it had burnt him. Even though he was being rude, somewhere deep in my heart I felt that Natas was a kind boy.

Anyway, after a few minutes of cheering and laughter, everyone left me alone in the dormitory and went downstairs. I did not know why they went down, maybe for breakfast or exercises. I didn't have any energy to think either; all I could do was lie in bed remembering my grandfather's words: *Things are not always what they seem, even FEAR.* Remembering these words, I fell into a deep sleep until a whole bucketful of icy cold water was thrown at my face. I became a popsicle for a few seconds but, as expected, nobody cared. The children were back in the dormitory and they just laughed again.

When I stopped shivering, I looked at who had thrown the water. It was the lunch lady I had seen the previous day, but she wasn't a lunch lady; the name tag on her dress said "*Warden:* Lamia."I knew the meaning of the name Lamia—a *heartless vampire who preys on children.* As the definition explained, she was genuinely heartless; I could see it within one day of my stay at the orphanage.

Her voice stopped me from thinking about her personality. She said, "*Hey you, do you think you are the prince of Hemasise? Come on, get up and go down and join the troop.*"

I asked, "*What troop?*"

She rudely said, "*Stop asking questions and just follow my order! Go and join the drill.*"

I requested the warden, "*Please, my stomach is upset because of the smell, and I can't stand all by myself. How will I join the troop? Can't you please spare me for today, or please call a doctor to check on me?*"

Lamia glared at me. "How dare you! *Go down this instant! This is my orphanage, do you hear, and I am the head of it. All you're supposed to do is follow my orders!*" she barked, and then she walked off.

I got up from my bed with a little difficulty, slowly walked step by step, and finally managed to reach the troop. All the other kids were already standing in a line, and I was pushed into it.

Maybe my grandfather or my parents were watching me from heaven, or my pain reached the higher officials—there was a health checkup van, and the officials were checking everyone's pulse after their drills, one by one, to ensure that they wouldn't become weak during the annual ceremony parade. I heard two children talking; one said to the other that whoever was in good health could participate in the yearly ceremony of Hemasise, and if we performed well, our orphanage would get funding. The other child answered, "Yaa, I know about the health checkup, and our warden is very keen about getting funds."

Plucking up my courage, I inquired, "What is the reason for the annual ceremony and why is Lamia so enthusiastic about it?"

No one replied, but after I asked again and again, a teenage boy I'd seen in my dormitory looked around furtively and walked toward me.

CHAPTER II

"GLORY" OF HEMASISE

After a few seconds of silence, the teenage boy said, "The annual ceremony is *on that proud day of Hemasise: the glorious, empowered, supreme leader, chief commander, Supreme Commander's birthday."*

"Wait a minute," I interrupted. *"Why are you adding so many titles to the leader?"*

Before I could even complete my sentence, the teenage boy placed his hand on my mouth and whispered angrily, *"Don't you dare utter any more words about our supreme leader and chief commander. If you call him by his real name then, along with you, we will also fall into a terrible problem. The Supreme Commander's soldiers will cut off our tongues and sell them in the market. And if they know that you are inquiring about the Supreme Commander, they will slowly scrape your skin off. And if we answer your inquiry, we will be kept in the horrible dungeons, where we won't get any sort of food and we will get water only once a week. They will tie our legs with big, big chains, and if you dare to criticize him, you will be publicly executed, and the person who heard the criticism will have their ears cut off.*

"They are so cruel, they will thoroughly check whether you are dead or not. Once you're dead, the officials will dress you up in rags soaked in oil, and they will parade your body around the country so that other people don't even dare to say anything."

Scared, I said, *"Aaa … OK … OK … I … I … I … w …w … will never even dare to s … s … say anything or even think about our proud, glorious, empowered, supreme leader, chief commander, Supreme Commander of Hemasise."*

Hearing my answer, the teenage boy said, *"Good, you have finally got it. And we beg you, don't even ask us what else they would do; we have told you only half of it."*

My attention shifted to someone behind me who was breathing heavily. I looked back; standing there like the Grim Reaper was Seth. Squinting at me, he said, *"Don't you dare reveal to the officials what has been happening to you here. Remember that once they leave, you need to stay here in the orphanage."*

I sighed and stood still without answering him.

After waiting an hour in line, it was my turn for a checkup. The officials inquired about me. Before I could answer, Seth butted in. "He is a newbie in the orphanage. He takes time to adjust and we will make him practice all the prayers of the

Supreme Commander of Hemasise, and we will teach him how to write the Supreme Commander's biography." And the officials nodded approvingly.

I wondered, *What in the world? Only my parents and grandfather love me and no one else. Is everyone the same, with no humanity and no kindness?* I just kept quiet and went back to the dormitory.

CHAPTER III

EXPLORING THE ORPHANAGE

When everyone was busy with their chores, I decided to explore the third floor of the orphanage. Each end of the third floor was horrible and disgusting. There were mugs and buckets and other cleaning items for us to do our chores, but it looked like no one ever brought them to the third floor. The library was the only thing that caught my attention. I went inside and lost myself in aisles and aisles of my favorite books, and I gained a lot of energy by reading some of them. After some time, I felt I should go back to the dormitory because I might get in trouble for not finishing the list of chores allotted to me.

So, not wasting a second, I took a mop and a bucket of water and detergent, and started my chores. I tried to focus on my job, but the kids around me were always trying to get me in trouble. They kicked my bucket of water. My bad luck always leads the way; the water fell on the warden walking on the floor just below. Lamia and I exchanged looks; her face turned red with anger as she squinted at me, enraged, and she clearly thought I had purposefully poured detergent water on her head. But who would tell the truth? No one here supported me or understood me.

Lamia ran upstairs and tried to catch me. I tried to run from her, but I slipped on the detergent water. As I said, my bad luck always leads the way. She caught me and, instead of calling Seth, this time she dragged me herself into a corridor, the very same passage where Seth had taken me just a day ago. I thought I would get another visit to the Slime Room but, instead, she took me to the opposite room, which had a sign on it that read "Rat Cellar."

I began pleading. "Ma'am, please spare me. I didn't mean to do that, honestly. It was just an accident."

As usual, Lamia didn't listen. She just said, "Stay here for *24 hours with no food and no water,*" and then she ruthlessly slammed the door in my face and locked it.

The room was so creepy and so quiet that the silence scared me. I started to pace the room; my footsteps echoed across the room, breaking the silence. Then I heard a few noises. They weren't mine. They were high-pitched and squeaky. A small, gray creature appeared. It had a long tail and a pink nose. I felt it was cute and innocent—until it was joined by its companions and I had a parade of rats marching upon me.

I don't want to describe those 24 dreadful hours. Somehow, I was alive by the end of them.

Slowly, day by day, I was able to get the hang of life in the orphanage, but two things were bugging me—one was Natas and his friends who always tried to bully me, and the second was that I couldn't understand why the fourth floor was a no-entry zone.

One day I took my courage in my hands and asked Natas about the fourth floor and why it was a no-entry zone.

For the first time since I had entered the orphanage, Natas answered my question. He said, *"A witch stayed there."*

I gasped. *"Are you kidding? A witch scarier than Lamia?"*

I could see he didn't care for my response, but before he could say anything the horn of a vegetable truck began honking.

Seth screamed at us, *"You lazy beasts, come down and unload the truck!"*

Every time I wanted to ask Seth, *"Why can't you unload the truck? Why can't you do the chores? Why can't I put you in the Slime Room instead of you putting me?"* But I couldn't ask him, as I was alone. Everyone else would grab an opportunity to rat me out and get a good name in the eyes of that vile, nefarious Lamia.

Quickly, everyone got down to unloading the boxes one by one. Seth shoved my shoulder and said, *"Hey, you who thinks he's a prince—get a move on and unload the truck!"* and he winked at Natas evilly.

CHAPTER IV

THE EVIL PLOT AGAINST ME

I tried to be careful. Seeing their gestures and winks it was clear that they were plotting something against me. Still, to my shock, they were acting quite normal—until the exact moment when Lamia came out. That's when Natas tripped me by sticking out his leg in front of me and made me fall with a box full of vegetables.

All the vegetables landed like heavy rain on Lamia. I was sprawling right in front of her, in the open back of the truck, when her face got covered with tomato juice.

I got scared and jumped out and ran before the malevolent Lamia could punish me. I hid under the vegetable truck. How poor my idea was! The vegetable truck moved on and there I was, lying on the ground in the open with nobody to help me.

Lamia grabbed my neck and lifted me from the ground. She twisted my ear and dragged me (still holding my ear) into the dormitory. As usual, I pleaded with her but she didn't listen, and this time she gave me a different punishment.

"Clean the kitchen dishes for the whole week," she said with a snarl.

I was relieved as this was better than getting whippings or being in a rat cellar or being dunked in slime. The next day the weather was lovely and it started drizzling. The wind blowing from the kitchen window made me feel relaxed. The first three days went pretty well; I had no problem cleaning the dishes. I was enjoying the punishment this time with nice weather around me.

On the fourth day, the weather indicated torrential rain, but I ignored it and told myself not to think negatively and started cleaning my dishes. One by one, I washed and dried the plates and kept them on a platter. The moment I was about to leave, Natas came from the middle of nowhere and applied a lot of wet mud on the cleaned plates and mechanically laughed at me.

I hurried to remove the platter before Lamia could see it. I again washed all the dishes, and this time I kept them on the dining table.

The next day I was even more careful so as not to get any more punishments. I cleaned the dishes thoroughly and went to keep them on the dining table. But that's when Natas kept his leg in front of me and made me trip at the very moment Lamia was there. The plates went crashing down and I fell face first into a pile of broken ceramics, but none of the spectators cared about me.

This is great; what an opportunity God gives to them to make me punishable. Why has God made me like this, and nobody is there to take care of me? I asked myself.

I couldn't dare to look at Lamia's eyes. Roughly, she held me by the neck and said, *"I thought you were useful over here, but you are a waste ... unusable, filthy scum ... and you are misusing the valuable property of this prestigious institution."*

Institution? Seriously, what institution ... this is a house of horror. What are the kids learning here? Bullying, not caring for each other, making fun of others, I thought.

The very next moment, Lamia pushed me into the rain and said, "Spend the night in the rain. *DONT EVEN DARE TO KNOCK AT THE DOOR AND COME INSIDE TILL TOMORROW,*" and she closed the door.

By midnight I was drenched and miserable. I sat in a corner near the door. I hadn't eaten anything for hours. Finally, I felt so weak and faint that I gathered up my courage and knocked on the door. The minute I did so, I felt the dizziest I had ever been in my life. I started to wobble, then fell into a pile of wet mud and blacked out. When I woke up the next day, I was in my bed.

The obnoxious Lamia was talking to a doctor beside me.

CHAPTER V

THE ONLY "GOOD" DAY

My temperature shot up when I saw this scene. *Wait a minute,* I thought. *Do I see this for real, or is Lamia faking the meeting with the doctor? I wonder how a ruthless lady can call a doctor to take care of me and show pity on me.*

That's when I heard Lamia say, "Well, I need this boy to be walking. Reduce his temperature right now. No matter what medicine you give, make this filthy animal walk for the parade of our dear leader, the Supreme Commander of Hemasise."

But the doctor replied, "Ma'am, it's not possible. This boy needs at least a week of complete bed rest."

Hearing this, Lamia yelled, "Will you reduce his temperature right now, or should I break this useless creature's bones?"

The doctor looked worried; he must have understood the situation around me. He told Lamia that I would need to stay in a hospital for at least one day, and she had no option other than to agree.

"OK, look, Doctor Macharan, I need this boy walking by tomorrow when you drop him at the orphanage," Lamia replied and slammed the door as she left.

The doctor walked toward me with a smile on his face.

I thought, *I've seen him somewhere … where have I seen him?* I squinted and rubbed my eyes and looked at him again.

He bent toward me and rubbed my forehead lovingly. A closer look at the doctor made me realize that he was Dr. Macharan, who had taken care of my grandfather's health before he died.

I shakily asked, "A-Are you Dr. Ma-Macharan?"

He replied, "Yes, dear. The moment I entered this room, I recognized you and your situation. So, I just wanted you to get at least a day off from these punishments." He winked at me and said, "Keep it a secret between you and me. You need rest for at least one day."

So, I agreed to go to the hospital and stay there for one day. Oh, what a glorious day it was! I had the BEST food I had tasted in weeks. The day was excellent, yet it had to end. When I finally returned, I felt I was entering a lair of death and horror, which was my home.

I put my hand on the rotten-wood door, and I opened it to be greeted by the devil herself, Lamia!

CHAPTER VI

PROPAGANDA, PROPAGANDA

"Well," came her foul voice. *"You came back in a day, good! Now go to the English class in the library immediately!" Then she stalked off.*

What, this dreadful place has classes, and they teach academics? I said to myself. I got super excited because I love learning new things. I remembered my grandfather's words. He used to say, *"Things are not always as they seem, even fear."*

I ran toward the library. The moment I opened the door, my heart broke to see Lamia. To my shock, Lamia was the teacher.

She yelled at me, *"How much time do you take to come to the third floor, you filthy, foul animal? Sit down quietly!"*

I sat beside Natas. Lamia was teaching nothing that I had expected. I had thought they would teach English, Science, and Math, but there was no academics. The only thing she talked about was the parade next month on July 16!

"You good-for-nothing brats will march with the flags," she said, and she started talking all about it. The thing that annoyed me most was that Seth wasn't participating in the mile-long march!

I asked Natas why Seth was not participating, but he didn't reply. I wondered if Natas had not heard me, but then he passed me a chit saying *He is Lamia's son, now just stop asking me questions. If Seth thinks that I am friendly with you, I will be in big trouble.*

"But why?" I whispered to Natas. "Why would he spy on you and get you in big trouble if you spoke to me?"

"Enough. Stop asking me questions," Natas whispered back angrily. He started writing in his blue leather journal.

The whole day went by in propaganda and propaganda alone. The whole day Lamia made us write the biography of our Supreme Commander and glorious leader: lessons about his childhood, his fake victory over the city, and so on. As part of art & crafts, we had to draw his face and make art pieces with him in mind—artifacts promoting his glorious leadership. Using our artwork, Lamia tried to gain a good name and funding for running the orphanage, but she never used the funds for our benefit. Only she and her son, Seth, enjoyed the fruit of our work. Every Thursday, she made us do a demo march-past in front of the orphanage because it was the Supreme Commander's favorite day.

As my grandfather said, "*Things are not always as they seem, even fear.*" I thought they were teaching academics, but they were only teaching it in name. They showed us a movie every Friday night during dinner, but that was also about the Supreme Commander and his propaganda. If anyone deviated from this or spoke a word against it, they were severely punished in the name of the Supreme Commander— they had to drink sewage water and eat dirt for a week. And this entire movie-watching time was monitored by the fiend Seth. Since he was Lamia's son, he could do anything to us, and even if he didn't follow her ruthless rules, she would not punish her child. That was really unfair.

On one of the Fridays, when everyone was busy watching the movie, I sat with Natas as he was the only one who was at least answering my questions. Seth saw me sitting next to Natas, and he held my neck as if he was trying to choke me and dragged me to the other corner of the room.

He said savagely with a red face, "*NO FRIENDSHIPS ARE ALLOWED IN THIS HOUSE.*"

Quietly we finished our dinner, and while going back to the dormitory, Natas started to act uncannily as if he was my friend. He came close to me as we climbed the stairs to the second floor, then grabbed my hand and secretly handed me his blue leather journal.

He whispered, "*You will get answers to all your questions. Secretly open it at night and read it.*"

That's precisely what I did. When everyone was in a deep sleep, I opened the journal. The first few pages were about how Natas got to the orphanage, how he got settled, how he learned about Seth and his evil mom, but the thing that grabbed my attention was titled "*Year 5, Day 68.*"

CHAPTER VII

THE JOURNAL

Year 5, Day 68

A new kid, Yohanan, has the bed next to mine, and he seems very like-minded. He is so kind and so strong. He speaks confidently to everyone. I like him a lot. I want to make friends with him, with this beacon of kindness in a forest of rudeness. But if I do, Seth will keep me in the rat cellar. He will punish me till my death. I have had no option but to bully Yohanan and satisfy Seth's evilness. I plan to throw his trunk out of the dormitory window, to give the illusion that I am bullying him. I do not want to bully him, though. I have tried my best to tease Yohanan, but my heart has never liked it. One day I took courage and spoke to him nicely, tried to make a friendship secretly—but we were caught by the evil eyes of Seth.

Year 5, Day 83

Seth does not punish me as I am just a slave to him. He needs someone like me who does his chores unquestioningly, not someone like Yohanan, who is confident and strong. Yohanan questions Seth if anything goes wrong. This questioning attitude has made Seth try to get rid of him from the orphanage. He has punished him badly on several occasions. Yohanan was not served any kind of food for almost a week, and when he tried to complain to Lamia, Seth falsely accused him of stealing food, releasing the kids from the orphanage, and cracking escape plans. Yohanan was also blamed for talking about our vibrant democracy 100 years ago before the Supreme Commander took over the entire continent. The malignant Lamia obviously believes her son, Seth.

Lamia is eviler than her son. Hearing all the false accusations, she has handed over the wretched child to the officials of the grand leader and Supreme Commander of Hemasise. Yohanan has been taken from a small hell and put in an even bigger nightmare. I don't know how the officials treat the children they take away, but I have heard only scary and hellish stories from Lamia, the living witch. She told us that the wretched boy was executed, but I don't know. She could be lying; I hope so.

Year 5, Day 98

I turned the page to read what was next, and it was all about me. Natas felt the same way about me as he had about Yohanan. After reading it, I understood he didn't want to get me in trouble, which was why he was not answering my questions.

After reading his journal, I was even more scared to stay in the orphanage. I remembered my grandfather's words:

Things are not always as they seem, even fear. Natas wasn't what he had seemed like at first. Thinking about it, I slept with a heavy heart.

I woke up to the sounds of a truck horn.

CHAPTER VIII

NEW PUNISHMENT

It was our orphanage truck, the truck that brought items donated by the kind-hearted people of the city to the orphanage. The truck only advantaged Lamia and Seth, though. The kind people didn't know that only Seth and his mother got the fresh food and other good products while we children got horrible potato soup made from God-knows-how-old potatoes!

While unloading the truck, I saw a chocolate bar made by the best chocolate makers—"*Frandumburg's Best.*" It was on the ground. I picked it up when Seth and Lamia weren't looking, and I put it in my shirt pocket. Then I continued my work, pulling out a box of carrots and a crate of tomatoes.

Once I was done unloading the truck, I went back to the dormitory to admire the chocolate bar in its grand golden-black-blue wrapper. I really wanted to taste it, even though my instincts were telling me not to give in to the craving.

But it was irresistible. I stroked the silk-like wrapper and slowly started to open it. The golden-black-blue wrapper disappeared, revealing the layer of gold and silver that protected the chocolate. I slowly opened that too to see a tremendously tasty chocolate within it. It wasn't very special, but I hadn't had anything like that in months. I had barely got a nibble at it when I noticed a small boy pointing at me; he was no older than six or seven. And he was jumping up and down, out of control.

"Thief! Thief!" he yelled. *"I caught a thief! How lucky I am today! I will complain to Seth immediately. He will get you punished, he will!"* He took off down the hallway.

I froze at the mention of *Seth*. I knew I had to run. As I prepared to escape from the dormitory, I heard voices coming down the hallway. The voice of the small boy said, *"He who feels like a prince has stolen a chocolate bar!"* The voice of the evil Seth said, *"Good job! I will reward the prince immediately!"*

The small boy walked in, followed by Seth.

"Chocolate thief! You know very well that only my mom and I are allowed to have anything precious, and the only thing you are allowed to have is potato soup!" said Seth, menacingly.

I got out of bed and started to run! I ran like a lion was chasing me, but it was worse than a lion; it was the child of the most wicked person on Earth! And if I were caught, the consequences would be horrible!

While I ran, many thoughts also ran in my head. What will he do to me? Will he give me to the Supreme Commander? Or to the Department of Illegal Thoughts? Oh god … why am I thinking this? What have I done to myself? I need to find a place to hide. I need to think fast!

I ran up to the third floor. I tried to hide in the library, but I think the fiend Seth had a thousand eyes, because he found me between two aisles in no time. I tried to push the bookcases down on him, but I couldn't, and he was gaining on me whatever I did.

I didn't know why God was on the side of evil. I didn't know how a person could be so vile. I didn't know why all the other kids in the orphanage lacked empathy. I ran fast while thinking of all these unworthy people.

Think, Chris, think! I said to myself. The next second I saw the staircase which led to the forbidden fourth floor.

Should I go, should I not? Holding my breath, I decided to take the gamble. Rather than worrying about a non-existent witch's ghost, I felt I needed to worry about the real demon who was chasing me. I needed to save myself.

I ran toward the fourth-floor staircase.

CHAPTER IX

THE PHANTOM FLOOR

Seth shouted, *"Oh boy, you've crossed all your limits! You know you are not allowed to enter that zone!"*

That made me run even faster to protect myself. Pausing on a landing midway, I shoved two cupboards down the staircase to slow down Seth and have time to escape. Finally, I reached the fourth floor. I saw a can full of paint, and I quickly emptied this on the stairs to make Seth slip and fall.

Like the flip side of a coin, the fourth floor looked nothing like the rest of the orphanage. It was full of amazing things—all the stuff given by the kind-hearted residents of Pape was here. I was surrounded by new leather jackets, clothes, journals, and whatnot; it was sufficient for the entire orphanage for two years. I understood that wicked Seth and his nefarious mother, Lamia, had cooked up the story of the fourth-floor ghost so that they could hide and enjoy the precious items given by the people of the city.

Thinking of the devil, I heard Seth's footsteps coming upstairs, and he was saying the beep words which cannot be printed. He was biting his teeth and muttering to himself, *"If I find that filthy animal, I am going to choke him to death before he says anything. I shall punch him and drag him to the forest and give him as food to the man-eating vultures."*

I looked around for a place to hide. I tiptoed into a nearby room; it was filled with rusted metal furniture. Even though I was as still as a statue, the furniture made *creeeek-ity-creeek* sounds.

This thousand-eyed Seth figured out that I was hiding in the old furniture room. He said, *"Ahaa! I have caught you! You are such an innocent little dumb brat; you think I can't find you? I grew up here, and this orphanage is my home. I know it from end to end!"*

I did not know what to do; I did not know where to hide. No one was there to help. I had risked my life for a small piece of chocolate. And for the same chocolate, this detestable person was not acting like a human. I then saw a door leading into another room.

That room was dark compared to the other rooms. It smelled musty and all I could see was old, broken furniture. There were substantial canopied cots, the kind that were used in the olden days. There were several dusty, broken wooden boxes and broken cupboards with doors almost separated from their hinges. Carved tables and chairs with tattered upholstery, elegant but broken couches, marble busts (most of them cracked or broken), crystal, crockery items, and a whole lot of other stuff had been dumped in the room. A few moth-eaten carpets had been rolled up and placed in a corner.

The room had a dusty floor, cobwebs, debris, and a leaky ceiling. My heart thumped painfully inside my ribcage, and there was an upsurge of adrenaline in my body. For a brief moment, I couldn't hear anything. I started to feel that the whole place was eerie. The air grew cold and clammy as, step by step, I went further into the room. Then I heard the noise of Seth coming.

Where to hide? I thought. *And what to do?*

I noticed a dark mahogany cupboard hidden behind the rolls of worn carpets. Deciding to go there, I rushed into it. As I sat in the deafening silence of the cupboard, I began to hear noises from above. My spine was turning as cold as ice. I began to believe that there was a real ghost in the room. A musty, mildewed odor filled the air around me, and the smell made me sneeze several times. I put my hand over my mouth to muffle the sound, and then I tried to pull out my handkerchief, but I couldn't find it in my pocket. A shelf creaked ominously as I moved, and I sensed a black shadow coming toward me from above.

Before I could make out what it was, a metal object fell from the shelf above onto my head, and I thought I was dead moments before I lost consciousness.

CHAPTER X

AFTER A FORTNIGHT

I woke up feeling as if I had been asleep for a week. I felt a sharp pain in my head as though somebody had thrown a metal elephant at me. It was the third time I needed medical attention since I got to the House of Victory. But I didn't care about that. I was almost dead from dehydration and hunger. I opened the door, not bothering about if Seth would come and kill me. The door made a *creeeek-ity* noise, but nobody came. Maybe the ghost had eaten Seth and everybody else in the orphanage. However, that thought wasn't my priority; I was desperate to eat something. I felt like I hadn't eaten any food for a week. Feeling brave, I decided to go and eat food from the storage room, which I'd seen on the fourth floor. As soon as I left the furniture room, I felt scared again! I thought, *Will Seth catch me up here?*

Strangely enough, that devil, Seth, was nowhere to be seen.

I grabbed the nearest water bottle. The first sip made me so relaxed, I couldn't control myself. I drank the whole bottleful.

I then planned on eating the week-old Frandumburg's Best bar. But it had melted and I couldn't eat it, but I licked it. The moment I tasted the liquefied chocolate, I felt I was dwelling in a lake of caramel. Then I found some blueberry pie in a nearby oven. I gobbled it all up! To my wonder, nobody turned up and tried to stop me. I did not even hear any kind of noise around.

I wanted to go to the library downstairs, but I was afraid of Seth. Well, if he saw me, I could just run and hide in the cupboard again.

"Does Seth think I am dead? Why is no one trying to find me?" I murmured to myself. I took one step downstairs, then another, and then a third. I wasn't afraid of Seth now. I took five more steps, then a sixth, and then a seventh. After two more steps, I was in the library. I looked out the window and I saw dried-up, crumpled leaves rushing around the street.

The eerie silence was everywhere in the orphanage. I went downstairs to the second floor … there was nobody there. I looked in the dormitory, and there was nobody there. Taking a risk, I went to the warden's room; there was no wicked Lamia. I went to the Slime Room and then to the rat cellar, and there was nobody there either. It was as if the morning sun had sucked out the life of the place. I couldn't see Lamia or her son, Seth, anywhere in the orphanage. I went to the rotten front door and opened it. The main gates were wide open, and nobody was there. There was no sound of vehicles, birds, not even a bee; the only thing I heard was rushing wind with the crumpled leaves flying everywhere.

I walked along the street for a mile, and I noticed that nothing looked the same as before. The streets were deserted and the shops were empty. I searched everywhere, but I couldn't see anyone to talk to nor anything that would help me figure out what had happened. *Had I really been unconscious for a week, or was it more than a week? What had happened to the city? Where were all the people?*

A shop grabbed my attention—the lights were blinking! I ran into the shop, hoping to see human life, but it was as empty as the ones I had seen earlier. It looked as if someone had looted it. I left the shop sadly, all my hopes shattered. I walked outside, my shoulders slumped, my hands dangling as if they were held only by a thread. I sat under a large pine tree and leaned against it. What could possibly have happened?

I closed my eyes and remembered my grandfather saying, "*Things are not always as they seem, even fear.*" The shop was not as it seemed; I had thought some human life existed there, but it had turned out as barren as the other shops I had visited.

Thoughts flooded my mind. *What has happened to the city of Pape? Where are the Hemasiseian officials? What has happened to the evil Lamia and her son, Seth? What has happened to the orphanage kids? Where is Natas? Where is everyone else?*

Did anything happen? Did an earthquake hit the city? Did a tsunami come, and everyone was washed away? How did I survive? I was unconscious for only a week, I think; what major thing happened that made everyone vanish? Did an alien spaceship come; did aliens take over the land and take all humans prisoner? Or did the enemy nation's dictator launch a nuclear weapon?

Oh God, please help me … what has happened to the glorious city of Pape, which was once the jewel of Hemasise?

I fell into a sort of trance thinking about all the possible reasons that could cause the vanishing of the people of the city of Pape. The answer to all the questions in my head came unexpectedly. A newspaper, carried by the wind, came falling onto my nose.

CHAPTER XI

BREAKING NEWS

I picked up the paper and started to read it. The news blew my mind. The headline said: *Mutated Avian Flu, very contagious, mortality rate 99%.*

Ninety-nine percent! Thank god I survived! I said to myself. *That would mean only 1% of the human population is left!*

I felt worried. *Has everything happened in a week?* I quickly read on: *Mutated Avian Flu, a very contagious mortality rate of 99% … lasted for the past 14 days!*

How can I survive with no one around me? I need to find the people who survived this pandemic, I thought. Again, many questions arose in my head. *What if I get the flu? Will Pape City be safe for me? But where can I go? What day is today? How many days was I unconscious?* All these questions made me feel nervous and sick, and so scared that I couldn't stand up straight. I was feeling dizzy thinking of all this.

I heard a humming sound, which broke my flow of thought. Then the hum became a tune. The song was *Is anyone alive … is anyone alive … I want to see a human life … is anyone alive …* I rubbed my ears, not sure if I was hearing things.

The song was growing louder. I turned my head to see what it was but then closed my eyes. I didn't dare to see because my thoughts were stopping me: *I didn't hear any noise or humming. What if it is an alien monolith, or Seth is alive and coming for revenge, or if it is a man-eating vulture!*

I yelled out loud, *"Why did I fall for that stupid chocolate bar? Why couldn't I resist my craving? Why did I go to that idiotic cupboard and feel that there was a ghost? Why was I unconscious for a week?"*

A voice spoke right into my ear. *"You weren't unconscious for a week."*

I got so scared that I opened my eyes immediately, and then I jumped up. I couldn't believe my eyes. I rubbed them 100 times and pinched myself hard. It was NATAS.

We smiled at each other and hugged as if we were trying to squeeze the life out of each other. After a few minutes of squeezing, I started asking questions back-to-back without any gap for Natas to answer.

"Calm down, Chris. I too have so many questions to ask you. *Let us sit together for a while and talk,"* said Natas.

"What happened?" I asked him. "Why is nobody here?"

Natas replied, "*That day when you were running from Seth, I tried to stop him from finding you. I gathered all my courage as if I was a police commander and tried to hit him … how silly I am! He was stronger than me, and he threw me upwards in a single shot from the third floor into a fourth-floor room, as if he was a baseball player hitting a home run. I fell unconscious. When I woke up, there was nobody there!*

"*I searched all around the orphanage, but there was nobody. I wondered if the witch's ghost had swallowed everyone in the orphanage. I went around the city trying to find people, but only a few were left. The pandemic had hit the city badly—only a few people were alive and were rushing to the countryside. I went to them and asked if they could take me. However, there was no humanity around; even the pandemic didn't teach them any lesson. They left me and went to the countryside.*

"*I planned to leave for the countryside by myself if I couldn't find any helping hand. Luckily, God made me find you. And you were unconscious for 14 days, not a week. How lucky that we Hemasiseians can survive for a long time without food and water!*

"*How about you, Chris? How did you escape? How come Seth didn't kill you? That day after seeing Seth's behavior, I felt he was a serial killer, and I felt sure he was going to stab you and slaughter you and send your flesh to the butcher and your bones to the man-eating vultures.*"

I stopped Natas. "*Enough of explaining how Seth could have killed me. It is more horrible to hear it than experience it!*"

Forgetting about our situation, we laughed together, cracking jokes about Lamia and Seth for a long time. Recovering from the laughter, I started to narrate my story and how I survived the pandemic.

"I tried my best to hide from Seth, and I entered a creepy room on the fourth floor, which was full of rusted metal furniture. I hid in a cupboard. After waiting for some time in the spooky closet, I shifted a bit to take out a handkerchief from my pocket, and a shelf moved and some metal object fell off it and came flying at my head! I don't know anything after that. I woke up today and I looked in the library, rat cellar, warden's room, and dormitory, but there was nobody there!

"Then I searched everywhere outside the orphanage to know what had happened to the city and the people. I then noticed a newspaper which said, 'Mutated Avian Flu, very contagious, mortality rate 99%'. And then I was scolding myself for craving the chocolate bar when you showed up.

"What to do now?" I asked Natas.

CHAPTER XII

JOURNEY TO THE COUNTRYSIDE

"We can try and go to the countryside," Natas replied. "I think there will be some people in the countryside. The only question is if they will accept us or not."

"How far away is the countryside?"

"As far as I know, the countryside is about three miles from here."

For fun, I asked Natas, "How far can you walk in one hour?"

"Two miles," Natas said.

"Well, I can walk three! We shall make it in two hours!" I replied.

"But I feel so hungry; I need food to move a single step."

"The fourth floor is a storeroom, you remember. We'll get some food and water from there!"

So, we went back to that horrid, ghastly human slaughterhouse, but this time we were cracking jokes and having fun. After we had eaten like kings, we packed some food and started our journey with hopes and dreams, thinking about the people living in the countryside near Pape City.

We spoke to each other about our future and cracked many jokes about the malevolent Lamia and her son. We didn't even notice when we crossed three miles and reached the countryside. But the borders were fully protected by the Hemasiseian government officials, who were checking everyone thoroughly.

They asked everyone about masks, gloves, sanitizers, and checked noses with long earbuds, which looked awkward. But they didn't wear any personal protective equipment themselves.

The thing that made us crack a naughty and very illegal plan was that the officials were checking masks, gloves, and noses, but they were not checking the car trunks or trucks. So, we planned to hide in one of the trucks. This time God was on our side; the officials didn't check the truck, and we made it into the countryside.

CHAPTER XIII

HURDLES IN THE COUNTRYSIDE

Entering the countryside made our hopes and dreams stronger. We went about asking a few shop owners to offer us a job. But all of them sang the same song: *Can't take a risk in this pandemic time, dear.* We then planned to get a job in agriculture, but all the farmers turned up their noses at us!

Once you are in the countryside, you need to find a job to get a place to stay. But nobody was kind enough to give us a job! Everyone was worried about the pandemic! We had no place to stay or sleep. So, we had to sleep in different places. We slept in the church the first night, and the following day when the church father found us, we asked him for a place to stay. However, he too sang the same song which had become a mantra: *Can't take a risk at this pandemic time, dear. However, he did offer us a job for one day, cleaning the church steps and hallway.*

The next night, we slept in a hospital basement in the company of rats and mice, and the following day we asked the hospital officials for a small job, but they chanted the mantra: *Can't take a risk at this pandemic time, dear.*

After that, we slept in a park, but the government officials came and chanted the mantra and kicked us out. Slowly, the mantra transformed into a greeting.

At last, we slept in the cemetery for a week, wondering what to do and how to lead our lives. We thought we wouldn't get any job in the cemetery, but we asked the elderly caretaker anyway. He led a humble life, spending each day cleaning the cemetery, removing the weeds. When we took our chance asking him for a job, luckily, he said, "*Dear children, you are too small to work, but my age is making me fall so I will give you the job. You can stay with me in my small hut. Every day make sure to clear all the weeds and greet the people who come in and go out.*"

Natas and I had *thought we would get a job somewhere where humanity was alive, but we found humanity where people left their bodies.*

For a month, we worked in the cemetery and stayed with the elderly caretaker in his small hut. We became a family, and we thought everything would go well.

Because of the pandemic, people were disappearing every day. Many came for the death ceremonies. Among them was the Accab couple. Mr. Accab was a short man, only 4'2". He had a mustache and green eyes, and he was very kind.

Mrs. Accab was the complete opposite of Lamia; she had a soft and gentle voice, like a hummingbird. She always wore the same earrings. Her hair was braided and extended down her back like a snake. She had brown skin and beautiful brown eyes, which I admired. She was just like an angel sent by a divine power. Mr. and Mrs. Accab were friendly, humble, and down-to-earth. Mrs. Accab always offered us fruit or some vegetables. They used to check on our health and needs.

Everything was going smoothly, and it was just perfect, but the Grim Reaper again made our hopes of survival zero by taking the kind caretaker's soul and our happiness. However, we gathered all our strength and continued working in the cemetery; we were already used to so many problems … the cruelties at the orphanage, the loneliness given by the pandemic, our daily struggles for food and a job.

Natas and I had a strong desire to study, but just getting food was hard for us. We were both dreaming of a fruit which we could never reach.

Natas said, *"Let's not think about the things we can't afford or achieve."*

CHAPTER XIV

THE ACCABS' SURPRISE

We were doing our jobs as usual: cleaning the cemetery, greeting the people who came in and went out. And, slowly, we were growing close to the Accab couple. We had a soft spot for them due to their kind nature. They even gave us tips of money whenever they visited. Seeing their friendly nature, we decided to ask them about their family and kids, and about who had died.

So, we asked the Accab couple, "*Where are your kids? Why do you come every day? Who died?*"

They sat down and answered, "*None of our family members have died, children. We just come here to offer our prayers to the families who have lost their loved ones during the pandemic.*"

"*Families who have lost their loved ones?*" Natas and I exclaimed. "*We thought we were the only people who ever faced such sorrows, and that there are no kind people in this world.*"

Then, they asked us, *"What sorrows have you gone through? Wasn't that old man who took care of this cemetery your grandfather?"*

We then explained our hardships. The evil Lamia, the difficulties we'd faced, how we were beaten up, the horrible potato soup that we were served every day, the punishments given by Seth, her son, and the worse punishments given by Lamia, such as being locked in the rat cellar, the chores, and being locked outside in the heavy rain!

Natas explained how the House of Victory had treated his friends, sending them off to become government slaves. Then we explained how Seth had chased us and how we became homeless! How we met again! How we crossed the border into the countryside! How we tried to get a job and slept in the church, hospital, and cemetery! And how we met the elderly caretaker, who had treated us with such kindness and whom we had lost! And most of all, we explained how badly we wanted to study!

As soon as the Accab couple heard about our struggles, they started to weep! *"Is this the way people treat innocent children? Children are on par with God; how can they do this to destitute children? We are so sorry, dear children, to see how humanity has been forgotten in this society and for what you have had to deal with at such a young age!"*

With tears in their eyes, Mr. and Mrs. Accab went aside and spoke to each other secretly.

We only heard them say *"poor kids."*

After their talk, they asked us, "*Dear children, can we ask you one question? We feel we have developed a close bond with you.*"

Natas and I answered together, "*Yes, ma'am. Why not.*"

They started saying, "*What iffffff…?*"

"*What ifff…*" they continued.

"*Ma'am, please don't keep us in suspense. We have already had enough struggles. Are you going to hand us over to the government officials and make us study there? Please don't do that; all they teach is propaganda.*"

They laughed self-consciously and continued with the same "What if …"

We said, "Ma'am, Sir, *please, enough suspense. Please reveal it. What if… what?*"

Mrs. Accab again laughed self-consciously and said, "*What if… I became your mother?*"

We gasped. "*What … What… How is that possible!*"

"Well, *what if we adopted you both and gave you our surname? You would be Natas Accab and Christopher Accab.*"

Hearing these wonderful, life-changing words, our minds were whizzing with thoughts around the possibilities of living with the Accabs. Without a single negative thought, and without hesitation, we both agreed to go with them.

And so, we all stayed together and made many memories. Natas and I got a lot of kindness and love, which we had rarely experienced in our lives. We joined the best school in the countryside and we had the best education, which we could never have imagined achieving. We studied hard and finished our academic life, and then we made our careers in reputed companies and cared for our God-given parents.

After all these years, I still always recollect my grandfather's words: *Things are not always as they seem, even fear.* These words were proven right many times. The orphanage wasn't nice, but without it I wouldn't have got a brother like Natas; the flu pandemic was awful, but without it we wouldn't have met the kind elderly caretaker and we wouldn't have become part of the Accab family.

Natas and I faced our fears and became more assertive in our lives, and I never forgot to sends thanks to my grandfather for letting me know the real meaning of the sentence *Things are not always as they seem, even fear.*